Here Over Here Over Here

Jacob Chapman

for my parents

Published by Human Error Publishing
www.humanerrorpublishing.com
paul@humanerrorpublishing.com

ISBN: 978-1-948521-75-8

Cover art by Rachel Chapman

Table of Contents

No

I remember my first refusal, the first time
I said no, I'm not going to read that.
Seventh grade, a terrible-looking book,
a teacher who brought out the worst in me.
I took my F like a man
and kept the unread book on display
in my room. I pointed it out to visitors,
who never knew what to say.
My grandmother shook her head.
I started wondering what was in the book:
battles, speeches about the dead, old-timers
complaining about vanishing ways of life,
farming tips, how to conserve your energy
during the harvest, how to overthrow
the government. I turned in a book report
summarizing my thoughts,
and my teacher said you don't understand
what we're trying to do here.
I turned in more book reports
for the same book, and even though
they were all returned with a red F
on the front page, they grew into a series
about the Civil War: vanished regiments,
kisses on the road, vague and widespread
heroism, vague and widespread defeat.

In the Morning

When I walked downstairs,
so many things were labeled: the faucet,
some forks, a glass of water, the floor,
all in my own handwriting. Great,
I thought, I'm sleepwalking again.
I checked the video from my helmet-cam,
and after fast-forwarding through hours
of darkness and the occasional mumble,
I saw movement and slowed the video down.
I watched as I got out of bed
and walked downstairs,
where I barked orders to no one in particular
and demanded the proper immigration form
because our plane had landed
and we were taxiing off the runway.
The form! I need the form! I said.
I fell asleep on the couch,
then I rose quietly and started writing labels
and attaching them to things.
I took a label and wrote *the ceiling, above that*
the attic, above that the sky and various patterns.
I taped it to the ceiling and walked upstairs,
where I slept without moving.
Light slowly entered the room,
so slowly it made the rest of my night
seem impatient and moody, so slowly
I watched it again and again
as my real day passed by.

Blue Lines

Let's go find a river, you said.
I'd been in a mood, and you could tell.

A river, I said. Yeah, a river.
You pointed to a blue squiggle

on the map and said that looks good.
It did look good. We hiked through the woods

to find it, and it was more of a creek
than a river. Downstream, it flowed into a cave.

Let's take a nap, you said. It's beautiful here.
No, I said. How could you sleep

near that cave? It's not on the map.
The blue line keeps going to the ocean.

So what? you said. I bought that map from someone
who changes maps with erasers and pencils.

This isn't a great time to tell me that, I said.
You laughed and said I've told you that

many times. I sat down and slowly remembered
you telling me about the map.

You're right, I said. You have told me.
I know, you said. Let's listen to the water

going into the cave. We did that for a while,
and then you said we're going in.

That's a really bad idea, I said.
We could fall, we could drown.

None of that will happen, you said. Come on.
I walked into the cave with you

because I owed you one
and because I couldn't let you go alone.

The Silly Crazyface Dance

You said you don't do silly,
but you do silly.
You do your silly crazyface dance,
the one with the wild,
vaguely threatening arm movements,
the one your old friends always demand,
the one that frightened and excited me
when I first saw it.
Well then, I remember thinking,
this girl's got some heat.
Remember when we drove over the state line
twenty times in one night?
Back and forth for no good reason.
We drove through stupid and funny
and kept going.
We ended up in a quiet mood,
and every lap seemed to put
another layer of night on us.
If we're pilgrims, as you say we are,
we're pretty lazy pilgrims.
I'm OK with that,
but if we're going to cross deserts
and mountains and seas
and loop around again
without making a mess of it all,
we'll need strength.
And silly.
And not silly.
And we'll need each other.

The Wedding After-Party

The party squatted down on the deck and said bring me another one.
I was a few steps away from the stairs, which led to my bed, my soft
soft pillow, and an amazing night of sleep. You're not allowed to go
to sleep, the party said. What are you, crazy? I was playing one of
six guitars, and we were playing two songs simultaneously. I made
out bits of the song I wasn't playing: *leaf (leave?) . . . Mexico . . . turn
around . . . get back to you.* I slammed my guitar into the other song and
it fit. I realized someone had been telling me, and only me, a story,
and neither of us noticed I wasn't listening until we both did, and the
story stopped. Loud, loud, loud out there. It's not our fault somebody
brought a baby. There was mystery blood splattered around the sink,
and everyone wanted the story. Everyone wanted to tell a story at the
same time. The baby was fine. The baby was awesome. When some-
one said the neighbors just called, we all laughed.

Renovations

What were we thinking, putting so many colors
in one room? We used every single color
to make a horrible splattered rainbow of a room.
And your idea of a transparent roof?
To watch the stars, to watch the rain?
Well, it was a good idea, even though
I prefer your idea of a dungeon
where friends could sleep if they felt guilty
or your idea of placing many small statues
of gentle and fierce animals
outside to guard the front door.
The friends we didn't scare away
would come in and say *What in the hell*
is going on with those animals?
Let's rein it in. It's your turn
to rein it in. Let's get out the paint
and the rollers. Or let's sleep on it,
let's sleep in the rainbow explosion room
with flickering candles, with open windows
and strange dreams we almost, almost remember.

You Have Questions, I Have Answers

No we can't build a crypt in the basement.
Yes doctors cut up dead people in doctor school.
Yes it's legal, but it wasn't always legal.
People used to steal bodies from cemeteries
to cut them up and see how they worked,
so cemeteries had guards at night.
Yes being a security guard is boring
except when it's not.
Yes animals sometimes kill each other.
Yes nature is confusing.
Yes dying in a tornado would be bad.
But it would be quick.
A glorious death? I'm not sure about that.
I'm not sure I'd call that death
or any other death glorious.
What have you been reading?
Yes drowning would be terrible.
Yes being lost at sea would be terrible.
Yes I suppose you could be rescued
by dolphins, but I wouldn't count on it.
No I'm not trying to crush your dreams.

My Birthday Party

Everyone's getting a red wig and silver nail polish
whether they like it or not. And black mascara.
Then we'll go trick or treating, even though it's May,
and we'll hand out rubber snakes to people
who have no treats for us. And then,
because the parents won't be able to tell
which kid is theirs, they'll take the wrong one home.
But the food will be weird at every house,
and all the kids will say I don't want to be
in this family anymore. The parents will say OK,
and we'll all come back together, and the kids
will run in a circle, a blurry red-silver-black circle,
and we'll jump out of the circle in front of our real parents,
who will say you look different. And we'll say
stop being silly—it's just a wig. And the parents
will say I'm not so sure about that. Then we'll laugh.
Then everyone will go home, for real this time,
and we'll all say somebody's been here.
Somebody's been messing with my stuff.

Fortunes

The kids at the birthday party passed out envelopes
to the grownups, art projects with fortunes
the kids had written and drawn for us.
I did my best to avoid young James,
whose mind is filled with scenes of destruction
and who, one day, will become a master of something.
To my relief, he gave his envelope to another parent
who bent down, smiled, and thanked him.
Those of us without fortunes came together
in the corner, laughed and shrugged it off,
but we were a little sad not to be chosen.
We are men and women of destiny, I said,
we will make our own fortunes, we will speed
across the plains in search of punishing mountains
and canyons so deep and wide
they seem to be saying No. No. No. No.
And we will be quietly thankful
that we have to turn around.
My mind came back to the party,
and the rest of the not-chosen parents
were looking at me in a strange way,
and I knew that once again I had been talking
talking talking, and not listening at all.

Spending Time with My Great-Uncle

My great-uncle said he knew a thing or two
about living through a revolution.
He had lived all over the world.
I asked him what a revolution was,
and he said what kind of nonsense
are they teaching you in school?
For him, everything was either worthwhile
or a waste of time. He always asked me
to summarize my recent activities.
Reading—worthwhile.
Playing with friends—worthwhile.
Learning math—waste of time.
Learning ice skating—waste of time.
Learning to swim—worthwhile.
Learning Spanish—worthwhile.
Learning to sit still in the snow—worthwhile.
Very worthwhile.
After that one, he looked at me and said young man,
you're coming along nicely
despite living in this ridiculous town.
I told him he was ridiculous.
He laughed and said maybe I am. I grew up here
just like you. One day you'll leave
for some reason or another
and you'll drift through cities with towers
where the lights are never turned off,
you'll bet huge sums as the entire casino
cheers you on, you'll spend a year alone,
you'll be asked to join a group in the jungle,
you'll survive a bizarre incident
involving a goat and a river,
and you'll come back here and not quite know
what to make of this place, and it won't know
what to make of you. And that's OK.
It's one of the few places on Earth
where I can sleep soundly.
Whatever happens here, I can see it coming.
It can see me coming too.

The Resistance

When they dredged the lake for golf balls,
they found pills instead.
Thousands of pills.
Some had dissolved into paste,
but some were intact.
A retirement home was nearby,
and a group of residents
who called themselves The Resistance
admitted to pocketing their pills
and throwing them as far as they could
into the lake.
There was a state investigation.
Reporters came from everywhere.
In front of the cameras, the director broke down:
I love these people, but this job is so hard.
I don't know what to say. I'm sorry.
The leader of The Resistance told officials
he missed the feeling of lightness.
The official report was inconclusive
but ended by saying:
There needs to be a process
for dealing with the absence of loved ones.
They haunt this place.
They don't dot the landscape.
They are the landscape.

The Children of Southern Chile

Do the children of southern Chile
become delirious in the neverending
light of summer?
Do their northern cousins find them foolish?
I used to return from camp feral
smelling like mud and leaves.
We formed huge circles at camp.
We were always forming circles,
holding hands, forming circles.
Do the children of southern Chile
fall apart in the winter? I would.
My ideas would become tangled,
and I would join any tribe
if it promised to get me out of there.

Peloton

We were in the peloton
riding our bikes from party to party
at the First Annual Dia de los Muertos Ride.
I didn't know these people well.
The parties were brief, but something was burning
in the yard at every one.
A mattress, a sculpture, a car.
The parties exploded when we arrived,
but we couldn't stay long.
We had fifty miles to cover.
Most riders didn't know the rules of the peloton.
Our spacing was uneven.
We didn't speed up at the bottom of hills.
No one was using the right hand signals.
Someone slowed down too fast, and we went down
into a tangle of bikes and limbs.
Some wheels looked like tacos.
I heard someone moaning.
Everyone could walk, so we started walking.
No one drove by, and we slogged along
unsure where, or how, the day would end.

Teenage Boys Who Play the Guitar

Teenage boys who play the guitar
think your favorite band is lame
say *what's up?* to everyone
and argue about The Stones.
They want to start a band
maybe more than one band
achieve glory
then go solo.
They spend entire days in guitar stores
without buying anything.
They know that drugs are bad
but also somehow good.
One day, they'll know more
about music than their uncles
and their brothers combined.
They don't need lessons
but they secretly watch lessons online.
Their favorite bands are always changing.
They choose T-shirts carefully.
They daydream about going to a party
where someone hands them a guitar
and says *come on, man. Play something.*
People quiet down to listen
and the girls gather around.

Cave Air

The bubbles of the earth, the little caves
that haven't surfaced, have clear black air.
I'd like to take a hit of cave air in its purest form
and go to a party high on cave air.
I'm a hermit who knows
it's not always good to be a hermit.
I would take hits of cave air in the bathroom.
I would walk home high, mostly floating,
and the earth would vibrate and release
little bits of cave air from the ground.
I would look for the blinking lights
of the radio tower, and I would snap my fingers,
keeping time with the lights
as I tried to pull myself back down to earth.

The Capital

Our friend ended up in the capital
for the third time in a year.
We drove two hours to pick him up.
When we found him, he was laughing
in a crazy voice. My friend,
who used to ask me
if I still played the piano
if I still woke at dawn
if I still drank alone too much.
Oh, if I could grind a layer off
the things he's done,
would he settle down?
Yes, maybe, yes, maybe, yes,
maybe, yes, maybe, yes, maybe, yes.

Dream Sleep

I've fallen asleep everywhere: in libraries,
stores, and boats, under beds and pool tables,
in the grass, on a roof, in the middle
of a movie, in the middle of a sentence.
Dreams. The few I remember
may not even be dreams.
They may be fake dreams my mind creates
as it wakes up and scrambles
to produce something at the last minute,
something to satisfy its own desires.
Sometimes my mind is stiff and logical.
I want it to loosen up at night
and give me a dream
with people I haven't thought about in years
speaking in a language I mostly understand
sitting in a garden that feels familiar
talking about the things that deceive them:
fear, the endless versions of pride,
the need for symmetry, old age,
and the pleasure of being mildly deceived,
without consequence, for just a little while.

Poem to Make You Levitate

Giant ants took over my house, three and four
feet long, and when I came home, they said

You're back, come in, we have some issues
to discuss with you. I said OK

and waited for more of an explanation.
Hydramethylnon pesticide was a poor choice

they said, but you couldn't have known. We train
by eating small, then increasing, portions

and gradually, this happens.
I tied myself to the chair, like Odysseus

passing through the sirens' greenish hair.
I knew I couldn't leave the house

and I couldn't let this conversation stop.
I couldn't feel my feet as they slowly pushed

small creak, small crack, some tipping now,
through the floor the ants had eaten away.

Again

I tried to kill it every night.
At first, I let it rummage around
as I pretended to sleep. When I did drift off
I only dreamed of lying on my bed awake.

It pulled my hand one night at 2 A.M. and said
Wake up--I'm bored, and I can't sleep.
Where was I supposed to go?
It pulled my hand again and said wake up.

I knew it wasn't leaving when it told me
You get the day, I get the night.
We never had a deal.
I drowned it, cut it, threw it out the window.

It came back. In better moods,
we stayed up playing chess. It always won.

All Sorts of Things

I went to the river everyday for a month
to think, to let my mind drift around.
I didn't go to work for a few days
just to see what would happen.
I paid half my rent for the same reason.
My days sagged in a strange way.
Who would vouch for me now? I wouldn't.
I sewed some money into my jacket
for no good reason. I still don't know
why I did that. I walked around town
in the middle of the night. A homeless guy
challenged me to an arm-wrestling contest.
He won, but it was close. I think. Maybe
he was humoring me. We laughed
about nothing in particular.
I walked home. The next day,
the world seemed a little less blurry.
I hadn't been dreaming, but it felt that way.
I wanted a ledger with crisp rows and columns.
I wanted to do some arithmetic,
which I've always found to be calming and orderly.
The numbers distract me from my musings,
which is a quaint word that perfectly
describes my thoughts. I'm bringing it back.
I'm bringing back all sorts of things.

Mud Season

I forgot I had an ice cream cone in my hand.
It melted all over my fingers
and dripped down onto the marble floor,
which was beautiful but out of place
next to racks of baby T-shirts that said "I'm a Lucky Little Devil"
and walls covered with wood paneling.
Nearby, a group of teens started shaking,
bit their tongues, and yelled *John is the cutest!*
They could've torn my face off if they wanted to.
People kept coming in
taking up space and making noise.
So much talking.
I wasn't going to talk to anyone.
I still had some melted ice cream
in the bottom of my cone.
I drank it (delicious) and smeared chocolate sludge
all over my face
so no one would mess with me.
I walked to my car and no one messed with me,
but they were probably distracted, as I was,
by the horrible state of the parking lot,
which was nothing but mud.
My boots made weird sucking noises with every step.

The Bats, The Bats

When the dumptruck arrived
and the driver said where do you want the sand,
I told him I didn't buy any sand.
I know, the driver said. Your buddy did.
It's a gift, and it's the best sand there is.
Bats flew by overhead, and I remembered reading
they were headed south for the winter
to burn the fungus off their fur.
The only friend who would buy me sand
knows I can't say no to anything free.
Alright, I told the driver.
I'll figure something out. Just dump it all
in the backyard near the basement door.
I shoveled it around, and in a few hours,
I had an indoor beach and an outdoor beach.
Bats kept flying over me.
I inflated a kiddie pool in the basement,
cranked the heat, and scrubbed off in the pool.
Jars of jam lined the shelves.
I felt like I was prepared for anything.
I opened the door, and the bats,
the bats flew by
in their twitchy, zig-zag way.
I hope they make it to the desert, I thought,
or at least somewhere hot, somewhere
with sand and salt. If they don't,
the fungus will hold on—a little here, a little there,
enough to wipe them out.
The bats, the bats flew by
and no matter what I tried, I could not relax.

The Opposite of Vandalism

The drive-in movie screen stayed white
after the theater closed
and weeds took over the parking lot.
I thought the screen was bleached by the sun,
but one day I drove by, and the screen
was so white it made me squint.
I pulled in and walked up to it.
There were fresh drops of paint
scattered on the ground.
Why would someone do that?
To preserve old memories?
To show their own movies late at night?
The owner lived in a nursing home
and wouldn't meet with me.
I asked around about the screen,
and no one else had noticed.
Why do you care? my friend asked me.
I don't know, I said.
It happened again and again,
fresh layers of white paint without an explanation.
I spent an embarrassing amount of time and energy
trying to find out who was painting the screen.
I camped out within sight of it.
I annoyed everyone at every local paint store.
I brought my friend to see the screen up close
because I knew he would listen to my endless rambling
even if he didn't care what I was talking about.
Maybe it's time
to move on to something else, he said.
I stood there for a minute.
Maybe it is, I said. Maybe it is.

The Video Project

The grad student I hired
to follow me around and film my days
would rather be somewhere else,
but he does his job.
His name is Brad.
The whole thing started
when someone sent me a check in the mail
with a note that said Nice job—keep it up.
Keep what up? I asked myself.
I barely do anything.
So I'm recording my days
or Brad's recording my days
so I can keep track of myself.
Going through the video is exhausting.
Sometimes the video is just me
sitting there watching video.
There's me getting groceries.
There's me walking through town,
making small talk with Brad.
There's the guy who always comes up to me
and says Hey buddy—what's with the camera?
What are you? Famous?

Under the Ridgeline

It's about to rain, and the blueprints,
the blueprints will be ruined again.
Once again I feel trapped in a dream
where I make the same mistakes over and over:
I don't check the weather, I don't look at the sky,
I don't bring a raincoat. Here,
under the ridgeline, is a rare patch of flat ground
where I could build a house.
A widow owns the entire mountain,
and I want it, I want it all,
but I've learned to tame my greed.
She won't sell, not even a little bit.
I've flattered and bribed her from every angle,
but nothing works. So I come here uninvited,
to the flat spot beneath the ridgeline,
and I get rained on, and I go home, and I try
to develop other interests, I try to find new places,
but I still wake early, pack my bag
while I'm half-asleep, start hiking,
and by the time I really wake up and realize
what I'm doing, I'm almost there.
I keep going, and I tell myself
I don't know what I'm doing.

Walking in the Woods

The hike we were considering
looked interesting on the map,
but it also looked too easy.
So we made rules to make it harder:
no water, no food, no trails.
Just the map.
We hiked for a long time.
My legs became numb,
and my thoughts flattened out.
When we met the hunter,
we were so exhausted we laughed.
He didn't. We disagreed
about where we were on the map.
He said Good luck, I'm outta here.
We tried to say No! Come back!
We've been coming here
since we were kids.
But we were so tired
it came out all wrong.
We said There are kids that come here,
and we're those kids.
The way out of here,
it's over that hill. Come with us.
He stared at us, and I knew
we had failed.
I knew if he didn't make it
out of there, it would be our fault.
Our rules, our stupid rules.
We could help ourselves,
but that was it. Everyone else
was on their own.

The Cowboy and the Shipwreck

When the ferry ran aground,
everyone turned to the cowboy,
who was stern and quiet.
Everyone asked him questions at the same time.
No one could stop talking.
No one could stop talking.
The cowboy took a pull from his flask
and said *This is pretty much what I expected.*
Everything slowed down,
and the bartender brought out trays
of Kool-Aid and vodka in plastic cups.
The cowboy shook his head
when he was offered a drink.
Everyone developed a swagger
and their own unique accent,
each of which was vaguely earthy.
The mood lifted.
Yay for the cowboy! everyone cheered.
Yay for the cowboy!
The ferry started to sink a bit,
and someone said something garbled
over the intercom.
The cowboy pointed out some boats
on the horizon.
Whaddaya think, cowboy? everyone asked.
The cowboy said *Look closely.*
They're getting bigger. They're coming toward us.
Everyone moved in to hug the cowboy,
who said *That'll do. That's plenty.*
That's close enough.

Best Mayor Ever

I could shave my head
and tape my hair back on
for Halloween, but no one likes it
when the mayor does things like that.

I can't forget that I'm the mayor.
The campaign was a joke, and it was your idea.
We went around town handing out medals
and naming corners after whoever was there.

We weren't supposed to win, but here we are.
I know you want out, but no.
You're the deputy mayor, and you tell me
where to go and where to sign.

The meetings, the meetings never end.
Bring in the kid who wrote my campaign memoir.
He fucked it all up, and the illustrations are terrible.
What was our slogan again? It was good.

Farmhouse of My Dreams

I want a farmhouse, and I want a good one.
I want it quaint but not decrepit.
I want a kitchen that smells like lasagna.
I want tiles with cool patterns.
A real farmhouse has a dirt floor basement,
but I don't want beetles and mice
running around down there
unless there's a terrible storm
and they have no place to go.
I want to be a friendly neighbor.
I'm going to practice scuffing up my grammar:
I'm doing good. I'm doing good. I'm doing good.
Oh, I can't quite do it. I keep grinding my teeth.
The basement. The basement would be hard for me.
I could be watching the sunset on the porch,
and there would be worms down there
tunneling through the walls
messing up the foundation
making the house tilt.
I would grow angry.
I would consider flooding the basement with concrete
after giving the worms a warning
with bright lights and loud music.
But the worms might think it's a party.
They would all come,
and I would have to say I'm not your friend
even though I want to be.

Water on the Brain

They say the water is bad.
They say the water will give you worms.
They say the water has chemicals you've never heard of.
They stand on the corner and take turns
holding a sign that says
What are YOU going to do about the water?
I was walking by humming a melody I couldn't place
when I read the sign and had no answer.
I pictured a man sitting beside a giant pool
at the water treatment plant
flipping through a magazine.
I closed my eyes and watched him
squirt a dropper full of fluoride into the pool.
And then I thought No.
There must be more science involved.
Crystal filtration, magnets, ultraviolet light,
ultrasound waves that break up everything
except the H and the O.
We were all standing there with water on the brain
when the sky opened up in a gentle way.
We leaned back and opened our mouths for a sip
as the rain dissolved us
just a little, enough to rest.

Flamingos at Night

I love the plastic pink flamingos
that line my street every year
on the third week of May.
As I drive past them,
I give them a little parade wave
and imagine myself
drifting through the applause
of a real parade
(thank you, thank you)
But at night,
as I drive by the flamingos,
their beady eyes
surprise me every time.
I slow down, and their eyes
become less beady
and more patient.
Recently I ate candy
and only candy
all day long.
As I passed the flamingos,
I stuck my tongue out
into the night
and said Look my tongue's blue.
I've been eating candy
all day long again.
I feel bad about it, a little,
but talking to you
is strangely calming,
and the night is young.

Clues

The neighborhood kids went from yard to yard
Looking for evidence, they said. Looking for clues.
Last month, an old man in a bathrobe
knocked on my door and asked me to leave.
You don't live here, he said.
His son caught up with him and brought him home.
Small piles of rocks have started appearing
in my yard. One pile stays, others come and go.
I can't tell if they're a threat, but I like them.
I move them around a little. Not too much.

The House on the Corner of 1st and Crescent

Gradually, the house seemed to shrink.
Fresh paint chipped off within a year.
People said the house was cursed.
The family living there went out less and less,
and all they ever wanted to talk about
was the Civil War and its aftermath.
People kept trying to help,
but conversations with the family went nowhere.
The town's founders would be embarrassed
by the entire situation.
They seem so practical and sturdy
in old photos, less susceptible to curses,
less susceptible to dreams.
No matter who died, the founders kept moving
until they stopped at this hilltop
out of exhaustion or because they said
This is it. This is the place.

Citizens

We should call the police, someone said.
No one had seen the old couple
for a month or more. We were considering
breaking down the door with axes.
An officer arrived and listened to us
without moving his head. He didn't take notes.
I couldn't tell how dumb he thought we were.
He said worst-case scenario, we break down the door
and find them dead. I was thinking about much worse
scenarios like gore and humiliating body positions
and an old man coming at me with a gun.
Give me an axe, the officer said.
Someone turned on a light inside,
and we scattered into the woods.
Stop running! the officer said. What are you doing?
I almost stopped, then I picked up the pace
and ran ran ran through the woods
over branches and fallen trees. I slowed down
to walk through a patch of giant ferns.
When I got home, the neighborhood was quiet.

The Year Without Spring

Not exactly, but pretty much.
One day—piles of snow, grumpy moods,
sledding, laughter. Then rain all night.
Seventy degrees in the morning,
snowball collections melted,
outdoor rock collections revealed,
organized by size/color/shape/purpose.
No peepers, just frogs. Frogs and old crocuses.
Some sulking about this, some confusion.
Coats put away, bins of summer clothes
pulled out. Flip-flops? Yes, flip-flops.
Too hot for Easter? Of course not.
But maybe. Everyone learning to speak
to strangers again, mangling small talk,
mangling grammar. No time
to ease back into it. Just hey hi hello,
what do you, how is your day, I mean how
was your winter? I mean that was pretty weird
what just happened, with the snow and the rain
and the rocks and the frogs and the heat.
How are your plans, I mean what are your plans
for summer? It was far away,
but not anymore. This grass is crazy high,
looks like it's been growing for years.

Snow in June

I ordered confetti, but they brought me snow.
In June. In a truck. It's much easier
to clean up, they said. It melts away.
I know it melts, I said. It's snow.
But I ordered confetti.
They shook their heads
as they shoveled snow into my yard.
We can make you into a snowman, they said.
I've never done that before, I said.
I put warm clothes on
so they could make me into a snowman,
which they did. It turned out to be
a hot day, and my new body
slowly melted off as I spent the day
looking around my yard
from the same point of view.
Why did I plant that tree there?
Those flowers are doing well.
The ferns are out of control again.
Animals came out of their holes
and took a good long look at me.
I looked back at them
until they had seen enough.
Off they went, back to their holes
and their practical concerns.

Playing Dead

Wrap yourself in gauze.
It sounds strange,
but it's a unique sensation.
Leave gaps for your eyes and mouth.
Wrap your hands last.
Go outside and lie down in the grass
near the sidewalk.
Look, it's a mummy
the neighborhood kids will say.
It's just me, you'll say.
Oh, they'll say,
What's that stuff all over you?
Ask them to pile rocks on your body
and pretend they're gems.
They'll do it.
Everyone likes to bury things.
Ask them to tell you about Egypt.
They'll know all about Egypt.
Tell them about the River Styx
until they have to go home for dinner.
Goodbye, they'll say,
thanks for the weird afternoon.
Goodbye, you'll say,
thanks for coming over.
Stay buried for a while,
then climb out of your tomb,
go inside, unwrap yourself, take a shower,
and sit there.
Turn out the lights
and sit there.
Whatever happens next
is up to you.

Facedown on the Common

The town common was filled with people
lying facedown in the grass.
I nudged one of the people with my foot.
Is this a protest? I asked him.
No, he said without looking up.
Well, what is it? I asked.
He didn't answer me.
I sat down on a bench
and watched a group of dogs
walk around the common.
Sometimes all I want is a normal day
with nothing weird. I reached into my bag
and pulled out a can of tennis balls.
I cracked it open next to my nose
and inhaled the strange synthetic air.
I threw the balls to the dogs,
but they ignored them and kept walking.
I joined them for a lap, then I lay down
in the common. I fell asleep
and woke up surrounded by mannequins
lying facedown. I noticed some people
mixed in with the mannequins.
Maybe the mannequins were always there.
I don't know. The dogs were still there,
slowly walking around the common.
I wanted to wake up again,
this time to yesterday,
which I barely remember at all.

The Outside World

In my free time
which is vast and unruly,
I track down different parole boards
and ask them what they would do with me
if I were up for parole.
Not that I'm in prison
or plan on going to prison,
but you never know.
After I've talked them into hearing me out,
which usually isn't that hard,
they ask a lot of questions.
They're curious, and so am I.
I review my recent projects
and activities, the ways in which
I'm bettering myself. They usually tell me
I'm not ready for the outside world.
They're wrong, of course,
but I enjoy watching them deliberate.
They're very serious, and they have absolutely
no sense of humor.
I thank them for their time
and walk out of there a free man,
lighter than before.
On these parole days,
I usually don't make plans for the rest of the day.
I walk around town
playing with house money.
I buy strangers drinks,
I throw money on the street,
I have unusual conversations.
The world's a big place,
and you have to see it to believe it.

After the Scandal

Ruined. People say I'm ruined.
I made a bad decision
or maybe the same bad decision
multiple times.
I don't feel ruined.
I know my decisions were bad,
but I had my reasons.
Maybe not the best reasons.
Maybe I wasn't thinking clearly.
My best friend says
Don't do it
whenever he sees
a certain look in my eye.
I usually say don't do what?
and he says you're about to make
one of your bad decisions.
So what? I say.
He says I love you,
but you're an idiot.
One day I'll say
I used to be such an idiot,
but those days are behind me.
Now my decisions are better
for the most part
and a little more boring.
I'll sigh and think of the good old days
of bad decisions.

Jump Up On It

Friend, have you been banned
from certain birthday parties celebrations Thanksgivings
county fairs sporting events?
Were there some bad manners involved?
Maybe? Some yelling?
Have you stolen things that didn't need stealing?
Have you thrown stuff around and caused a ruckus?
Have you called bullshit one too many times?
Well quit your fuming and call Big Jimmy.
I'm like a lawyer but better.
I help smooth shit over.
I'll help you apologize in your own words.
If you don't mean it,
we'll figure out some other words.
Friend, ain't it time for something like this?
Even if you're bulletproof?
Even if they've been screwing you over
from day one?
Might you shoulder some of the blame?
How about it, brother?
Jump up on it and tame yourself.

Party at Jackson Park

This Saturday, from 4 to 7 PM.
Bring whatever you want: juice, snacks,
dinner, beer, frisbees, footballs.
You can write down your burdens
(even the delicious ones)
and put them in a box that we'll provide.
We'll also have a stage
for people to do their thing.
Don't scare the kids.
We'll have other boxes for terrible decisions
you almost made and those you did.
We'll read some of both from the stage.
Then we'll plant a tree.
Everyone will get a handful of dirt.
We'll have the kids stomp it down.
We'll water the tree and pack up our things
(including our burdens, which don't go away
just because you write them down).
We'll drive home thinking about the power of luck,
the sheer variety of ways a life can go haywire,
the tree we planted, and the decisions we made
that weren't even decisions—
they were just things we did, stupid things,
embarrassing things, cruel things
we would never write down in a million years.

The Adams Foundation

For free rent, I moved into an apartment building
owned by The Adams Foundation. We were told
research would be ongoing but unobtrusive.
They rearranged my furniture while I slept.
Sometimes they changed my food, my clothes, my books.
I assumed there were cameras everywhere,
but after a certain point, they were rarely on my mind.
The daily survey included space for drawing.
Gradually, the changes they made in the nighttime
shifted things back to the way they were
after I moved in. My year there was coming to an end.
More than anything else, I wanted to see my file.
My worst fear was that there was no file.
Maybe the changes in the night were a distraction
from the real research, which I never noticed.
Maybe the space for drawing was there
to keep us occupied, to make us feel that someone
was keeping track of us. Oh, I didn't want to leave!
I didn't want to leave, and I still want my file.

Mapping the Marsh

Before we mapped the marsh, we spread Vaseline
on ourselves to stay warm and packed our supplies:
binoculars, paper, pencils, measuring tape.
We told no one where we were going.
There would have been too many questions.
We knew what we were doing.
We knew we would have to apologize.
We cut our palms and slapped them together.
In the marsh, we sprinkled glitter all over ourselves
and the sculpture we made with sticks and mud.
It got dark. We started yelling. Our neighbor,
a decent man, looked terrified when he found us.
I still see him sometimes, and I can tell
he thinks something will always be wrong with me.

Roadside Manners

The powder sprinkled on our food,
all our food, at the blue restaurant
made everything taste obscure and delicious.
Our waitress was so intimidating
we didn't ask about the ingredients.
We asked if they sold it
as some restaurants do,
and our waitress laughed and said
that's ridiculous.
We said why is that ridiculous?
You people, she said. You people.
The only building for miles,
and this is what we got.
There was no light in there,
just low windows, burned-out bulbs,
and grizzled regulars staring at us.
We licked our plates
because at that point, fuck it.
We left quickly, before the mob
realized it could be a mob,
but after saying thank you
and leaving a generous tip.

Checking In

The phone was ringing
next to the receptionist,
who was asleep in his chair.
I'd been standing there for a while,
dazed from a long drive.
Sometimes I do that. Stand there
and let things happen or not happen
around me. I wasn't in a rush.
I walked around the lobby
and picked up a book titled
Guide to the Eastern Woodlands
from the welcome table, which had a sign
that said *welcome table* in lower case letters.
The term eastern woodlands
seemed a little broad.
The phone started ringing again,
and a man walked into the lobby
wearing a bathing suit. He picked up the phone,
said *front desk . . . mm-hmm . . . you're welcome,*
hung up, saw me, said *why wake him?*
and walked away. Good point, I thought.
I took a room key and left a note
that said *I took room 17—thanks.*
I went to my room, took a shower,
toweled off, and my phone started ringing.
I knew it would take forever
to explain why I took the room key,
so I let the phone ring.
I was basically asleep anyway. More or less.
I envisioned my friends sitting there,
shaking their heads at me,
asking me what I was doing,
asking me how far
I was going to drift this time.
Not far, I said out loud.
Not far at all. I'll tell you when to worry,
but for now, I'm fine.

Water Rights

Let's say you're a civil servant
in a stubborn, isolated corner of the earth.
An old lady shows up
at all the county meetings
and says *I have foreseen it*
in the middle of mundane conversations.
Let's say you're mildly corrupt
not because you're ambitious or greedy
but because you're lazy
and saying no takes too much energy.
Let's say you become even lazier
and neglect your official duties
but no one notices.
Let's say you start caring.
You start asking for input at county meetings.
During one of your presentations,
the old lady says *they tried that in '62,*
but it didn't work because of water rights.
You hadn't thought of that.
You feel foolish, and you realize
your plan will never work.
Everyone knows your ancestors
bought up all the water rights in town.
The old lady walks you through the aisles
in the hall of public records.
She shows you your ancestors' files.
Some sections have been blacked out,
and most of it is hard to understand.
You get a headache and ask her
if she has a point.
Now you're wasting my time, she says.
You almost ask her if she has foreseen this,
but you don't
because you're not quite that rude.
She walks away, and you sit down.
You slowly look through the files
in search of something good
so you can stomach the bad.

The Man in the Mountain

If we follow this vein of silver
through the mines,
we'll find him sitting there,
his eyes completely black, completely dilated,
and it will be awkward. It always is.
Sometimes he throws things against the wall
and doesn't want to hear about the sunlight.
Sometimes he rambles about wisdom
and the things you can learn from metal.
Sometimes he asks to hear a story,
any story, and it's hard to tell
if he's listening or not.
You can hear water flowing through the walls
down there, and it can be comforting
or annoying, depending on your mood.
When we come home, people will ask us
What's it like? What's it like down there?

The Parade of the 1840's

People dress up and walk through town
in the Parade of the 1840's, one of many
local traditions with vague origins.
They smell like coffee, wax, and smoke.
They throw small wooden toys into the crowd
and ask for oranges. We throw them oranges.
They always say they're vitamin deficient.
They hole up for a week before the parade
and get all 1840's on everything.
They drink a lot and talk about abolition,
all the craziness going on out west,
and the wonder of trains and canals.
By the time of the parade, they're rowdy.
They walk through town and lift us up,
leaving us a little jostled and rowdy ourselves.
I never know what to do after the parade,
but some people know exactly what to do.
They drink homebrew and chop down trees.
The police hate the parade.
They moved it from the afternoon
to the morning to try to tamp it down,
but people didn't care. Nothing changed.
No one's taking away their 1840's parade.

The Town of Lemons

A couple walked by speaking a language
filled with x's and k's.
Where were they from?
What brought them to our town?
Founders Day, I suppose.
I followed them and their jagged sounds
up the hill everyone was climbing
on the edge of town,
but I lost them in the crowd.
When we all reached the top of the hill,
someone pointed to the river--
sailboats were moving back and forth
in a cluster. A gunshot!
The regatta had begun. Everyone clapped
and let the sun warm their faces.
I looked around and saw the couple.
I waved. They waved.
Welcome to our town, I said.
They stared at me.
Welcome   to   our   town, I said.
The sun wobbled in the heat.
Someone passed out lemons,
and everyone started eating them.
I looked away, toward the river.
Lemons. How can people eat them?
I come from the town of lemons,
and even during the rituals and joys
of Founders Day,
this caused me a small
manageable bit of shame.
The couple sniffed their lemons
and looked at me.
I took a bite of mine because, well,
I don't know.
This town will make you crazy.
This town this town of lemons this town
This town of lemons this town.

The Drought

I wore brown for a year
to support the local farmers.
There was a drought,
and even though I still wore other colors,
I always wore a little brown.
Most people didn't notice.
When I pointed it out and explained myself,
most people laughed, including the farmers.
I thought about changing my color
or my cause, but I couldn't stop thinking
about the crops and the farmers.
I helped quietly. I bought more food
than I needed at the farmers' market
and gave the rest away.
I put money in farmers' mailboxes.
You know you're weird
when you start doing things like that.
For months. And months.
And then the rains come, and the crops
come back, and wearing brown
seems morose, and you pause
because you don't know
what to do with yourself
now that everything's green again,
and you remind yourself that no one
knew what you were doing anyway.

Our Sister Country

After I visited our sister country,
I filed my report and rested my mind.
The people there were so polite
I could never tell what they were thinking.
Their coins have foxes on one side
and women surrounding foxes on the other.
I miss the way they pause at noon
no matter what they're doing.
I miss learning about their system of exile,
which is semi-voluntary,
rarely permanent, and among many
a source of civic pride.

The Terrible City

As I passed through the terrible city,
a million bodies pressed up against me.
On the street, on the subway,
in the park, everywhere.
They were everywhere, all kinds of people.
Men in suits, drunks, old women
who looked like they had lived through wars,
kids too young to be out there alone.
I say I passed through, but it was a slow
passing through. There are entire months
I barely remember.
I spent days riding The Big Loop,
the subway line around the city.
One lap took five hours.
On two-lap days, I saw some people twice—
they hadn't moved from their spot.
They were sitting on a bench, standing against the wall,
playing their guitar, talking to themselves.
Three-lap days felt wasteful and embarrassing,
but four-lap days were different.
By the fourth lap, my mind was pretty empty
and things just happened:
I held someone's baby for a minute
while she dealt with something,
I talked with a guy who had spraypainted himself,
and I asked some nuns about the devil.
They said they hadn't thought about the devil
in a while, and I didn't know what to make of that.
My year in the terrible city was coming to an end,
and I had no idea what to do with myself.

From Point A to Point B

Point A could be anywhere,
but our point A has canals.
And art. And buildings that don't mind water.
We eat things that repel and delight us.
In the meantime laughter.
In the meantime wine.
We hear jokes about us in another language.
We fire our guides.
We have a meeting and rehire our guides.
Tenuous understanding, tenuous respect.
A change of plans: point B is no longer possible,
is no longer, how do you say . . . safe?
Point C? An entire city based on hexagons?
OK. But our guides can't go there.
The group can't agree.
Excitement and fear.
And caution. And the need to return home.
Our guides decide to quit.
Unless we agree to go to the airport.
You're all crazy, they say.
There, in the distance, are mountains
that aren't even on the map.

Not Yet

Yes, we have to go back into the woods.
We've received our monthly package
but not our signal, a golden postcard
with no return address
and no written message.
I know your questions.
Who will send it?
On what conditions?
How do they know
that we're still here?
The details were lost in the fire
after our parents defected
from the rebellion
and settled here, quietly.
Presumably the war continues.
We can't risk sending scouts.
We have so many things here,
in our land of moss and steep ravines.
All this has been the case for many years,
and it's over when I say it's over.

The Silent General

He hadn't spoken in years.
He would stand over maps with his lieutenants
and go through hundreds of different scenarios:
moves, countermoves, sudden rainstorms,
the unexpected loss of provisions.
He tapped on important terrain.
His lieutenants learned his system of hand signals
but absorbed different lessons.
Sometimes they disagreed about his plans.
His aide-de-camp, a twelve-year-old boy,
was in charge of his alcohol.
The general threw things at him when he was drunk
and wanted more, but the boy would shake his head.
The next morning, the general would nod to him
and pat him on the shoulder.
After losses, the general took his knife
and cut another line on his cheek.
His men adored him. During one negotiation,
he scalped himself and held up his scalp
to his enemy. The skin grew back, the hair didn't.
He lost as much as he won, and the other generals
never knew what to make of him.
Later in life, he started talking again.
He tracked down his aide-de-camp
and poured him a drink.
He'd given up the stuff himself.
When he talked about the war, which was rare,
he didn't have a lot to say.
He avoided reporters and worked in his garden,
which had miniature landscapes
with mountains and rivers made of rocks.
Groups of animal and human figures
were arranged in different places.
Every spring, he leveled it and started again.

The Clearing

I could tell that everyone in town
knew where the mass grave was,

but no one would talk about it.
I found it using an old map,

and when I arrived
at the monument and the clearing

I had read so much about,
I felt sick. I had something to eat

and forced myself out of the car.
The monument was built by a man

who did nothing else for five years
and later shot himself in the clearing.

I walked out there and lay down.
I wanted to sink into the ground

or float into the air
or say something respectful

to the dead, but I couldn't think
of anything to say.

It was time for me to leave,
and it was time for me to let go,

just a little bit, of this place
that had taken over my life.

Time on Your Hands

A tunnel was discovered in our town.
It started in the basement of one house

and led to multiple rooms in a second house.
The original owners of the houses, Fogle and Smith,

were well-known enemies from the 1700s
who built rival empires of dry goods.

The tunnel had sturdy support beams
and a drainage system that relied on suction

from a nearby stream.
There was surprisingly little mold.

Under Fogle's house, different branches of the tunnel
led to the study, the bedroom, and the dining room.

I can see Smith trying one branch, then another,
figuring out where Fogel spent his time,

listening for clues, listening for plans.
Someone tried to convince me they were friends

or even lovers, but if so, why the different tunnels?
Both of them lived alone.

No, they were enemies,
and Smith was a committed enemy.

If you have nothing else to do,
this is the type of thing that happens.

First you build a cellar,
then you think I could dig a tunnel.

No one would know.
There's nothing stopping me.

Similar Doubts

As the armies passed each other
on their way to different wars,
they exchanged tokens and reports
of what lay ahead. The generals couldn't decide
if they were enemies or allies. They told their men
they were probably neither. The men relaxed
and talked about their different customs,
which seemed odd to the others:
sleeping with their dead the first night after death,
recording the position of the red star every night,
debating when and when not to feel lucky,
standing vigil over the dying, always burying them
on the southerly slopes of hills.
The generals traded candles and pens but not maps,
tried to decide if they were being tricked
by the other (probably not, they both thought),
wanted to tell each other their true mission,
which was the same: to settle a new colony
on the other side of the world
so their people could never be annihilated,
reminded themselves they could never share that,
and opened some of their best bottles of wine
to share with someone with similar tastes,
similar burdens, similar doubts.

A General History of Devonshire County, Massachusetts, 1674-1675

That book took over our lives. Devonshire County was real and lasted two years. The book presented nine different, sometimes contradictory histories, each in a different voice. One was a child's voice with misspellings and fantastical thinking. Another spoke constantly about fate and destiny. One was mostly about the food they ate, and another was solely a description of a game they played with blindfolds, sticks, and water. The publisher wouldn't reveal any information about the author or authors, who weren't named. There was no introduction. Some of it had to be false, but which part? The book was perfect for the internet: endless searching, message boards, blogs, conspiracy theories. The whole thing is still exhausting, but less so everyday. It's blending into our background, impossible to verify or disprove but there nonetheless, charming in its own strange way.

A Dutchman on the Delaware River, 1650

The Finns, who claim no land
but live wherever they like
are the hardest to gauge.
They clear land by burning it
and keep the fire going
by rolling burning logs around.
Our cares are not their cares.
We see them here and there,
dressed in furs, indifferent to us.
At least we understand the Swedes,
even though we'll never trust each other.
Lately, we can't find the Finns.
Did they move inland?
Did they return to their homeland?
Were they killed?
We walk through their dwellings,
still rank with their sweat and cooked fat,
and there is little left behind. Elsewhere,
our families drift away from us
and our dream of making a new world.
Their letters grow shorter
and tell us less and less.
If we can't secure our claims,
we'll have nothing to show for ourselves,
and no one will remember
that we were ever here.

Terra Incognita, 1540

A year ago, we crossed this river easily
during what must have been a drought.
When we reached it again last month,
we celebrated with a feast.
Our expedition was almost over.
Our ships were awaiting our return.
They still are, I hope.
Not that we found anything valuable.
No gold, no silver, no cities.
Just mountains and plains that went on forever.
The native people we saw
kept their distance from us.
Now the river is swollen.
We've been walking its banks,
and the other side is right there,
taunting us, driving us mad.
Two men built a raft and tried to cross,
but they were dead before they started,
and they knew it. They gave us their rings
to pass along if we made it home. I suppose
they wanted to get it over with.
I can sense a growing dissatisfaction
with me in the group, among some a growing hatred.
We're running out of food.
I've tried to convince them
that we should continue downstream.
We'll reach the coast eventually, and then
we'll signal a passing ship.
But I've lost their trust, and I don't know why.
Some have said there won't be a passing ship,
the only ships are our ships,
which are on the other side of the river.
Some mornings, we find that people have left
in the night. Sometimes I'm surprised
by who has slipped away.
Some of my best men, some I considered friends.
We have to reach the coast.
If we're going to die,

I refuse to drown in a river.
I'll die looking at the sea.

Back Channel

What is it about our two countries?
We came up the ranks together,
passing this country and that country
along the way, but we don't know each other.
Our country never learned how to cook,
but yours did. How did you do that, exactly?
None of you understand the first thing
about music, and you don't seem to care.
How do you not care about music?
And what is so confusing
about our holy relics? You touch them,
you feel something, then you move on
with your day. Your winters seem miserable,
but you love them. You don't understand
why our fog is so special to us.
It lets our minds wander,
and it allows us to rest.
We've both had defections to the other side.
Some painful losses, some massive misunderstandings,
like the one that brings us here.
Let's open a bottle and start writing a script
of what our leaders will say, and when.
It shouldn't be too hard this time.
Neither of them seem very agitated,
and they both want a way out.
This is mostly practice
for the times when we're all agitated
and war seems like the best idea
to everyone. Both of our countries
like to say Never submit, Never yield,
and that's a problem for both of us.

The Life of a Spy

Patience and sleep. What you need
is patience and sleep. You need
to seem smaller than you really are.
If you don't enjoy exploring
new foods and confusing traditions,
this life won't work for you. You will fail.
Torture is the thing we never talk about,
but it's always there, right around the corner.
I wonder what my country would exchange for me:
Decreased sanctions? A small island?
Another spy?
If the two of us were exchanged,
it would be nice
if we were given a few minutes alone.
What would we talk about?
Would we trade elaborate lies?
Would we sprinkle in random truths
about ourselves
so we could feel human for just a minute
with someone who's been
where we have been,
inside a neatly folded double life?

The Loyalty Oath

After we signed the loyalty oath,
we kept our heads down and shaved everyday.
Our names were posted.
The oath asked:
Do you renounce your beliefs?
Do you acknowledge that you have caused pain?
We answered yes and yes even though
we didn't mean it,
but the more I thought about it,
the more I meant it.
We both stopped sleeping.
I started to wonder
if we were on the wrong side.
I couldn't tell what you were thinking.
They separated us.
I read the book again and again.
Interrogator training began.
My trainer had a quiet voice.
Before I was ready, she said you're ready
and showed me through a door.
There you were, sitting at a table,
looking up at me.

The King Is Dead

Let's get out before they close the ports,
before people have time to think,
before the city turns against us.
We spent years becoming somebodies,
and now we must become nobodies,
specific nobodies with specific stories.
We have to tamp down our language
and tamp down our manners.
We can't go to Antwerp—
they'll be looking for us there.
We have to go east.
Venice. Venice is where we need to go.

Is this a bad dream? It seems familiar,
all these people running around,
the king dead, me talking, you listening
but not saying anything.
I feel like I've said these exact words before,
these exact words, these exact words.
Say something. Tell me I'm not dreaming.

Options

If we have to take the town,
let's sharpen our blades, drink a little,
and be done with it.
Of course they don't deserve it.
They're in the way,
and they would do the same to us.
May, my favorite month,
has never seemed so out of reach.
Whatever used to work
to keep the peace no longer works.
Maybe the lord mayor will reverse his decree
about grazing rights and property seizures,
but he probably won't.
Have you seen his eyes?
And if we take the town, then what?
The lords of the valley
would never support our claim,
and we wouldn't last for long.
It might be worth it,
just to be the first of our line
to hold the town.
Some of us would survive.
But I am old, and the lord mayor is ill.
His son is rumored to be merciful.
Maybe that is so.
You younger ones, with more to lose
and more to gain, must decide.

Some Time Ago

Across the water, coronations began
with the king-to-be walking alone
from the city wall to the central square.

Anyone could curse him
or strike him with a stick.
He wasn't allowed to speak or fight.

The road was always clogged with men,
women, children, sticks, and grievances.
The king-to-be arrived in the square bloody

and was stripped naked by the crowd.
He was cleaned and mended on a platform.
His body was oiled and dressed

as everyone watched. In silence,
the crown was placed upon his head,
and the king cried out

Ooo-lan, ooo-lan sani.
My reign, my reign has begun.

The Air Is the Air Is the Air

Sometimes
as we trim the extra off our lives
we hold something up to the light
and think what is this?
I don't remember this at all
it's a box I must have made
there's nothing inside
it looks like something
I would have made
and then we try
we try hard to remember
and if you try hard enough
you'll remember something
even if you find it floating in the air
and after you mold it
you can toss it back in the air
it will hover in front of you
you can place it inside your box
and then you have it
you get to keep it
it's yours again

Acknowledgements

Thank you to the editors of the journals where these poems were previously published: Common Ground Review: "Time on Your Hands"; Cruel Garters: "Best Mayor Ever" and "Our Sister Country"; Forklift, Ohio: "In the Morning," "No," "The Bats, The Bats," and "The Cowboy and the Shipwreck"; Naugatuck River Review: "The Town of Lemons"; and Meat for Tea: "Farmhouse of My Dreams," "Flamingoes at Night," "My Birthday Party," "Spending Time with My Great-Uncle," "Teenage Boys Who Play the Guitar," "The Outside World," "The Year Without Spring," "Walking in the Woods," and "You Have Questions, I Have Answers."

Thank you to the editors of Open Country Press for publishing several of these poems in the chapbook Other Places.